# The Lord's Prayer
## Study Guide

six-session series on
Jesus' blueprint for prayer

## Roger Street

**kevin mayhew**

First published in 2005 by
KEVIN MAYHEW LTD
Buxhall, Stowmarket, Suffolk, IP14 3BW
E-mail: info@kevinmayhewltd.com

9 8 7 6 5 4 3 2 1 0

ISBN  1 84417 338 0
Catalogue No.  1500751

Cover design by Angela Selfe
Edited and typeset by Graham Harris


Printed and bound in Great Britain

# Contents

*For my wife Heather,*
*'a pearl of great price'.*

# Running a small group successfully

Here are some straightforward guidelines to bear in mind when leading a small group. Many are simple but can easily be overlooked, so it's worth reminding yourself about them with a quick scan through before embarking on each session.

- Plan to involve everybody in some way. Ensure one voice does not dominate, particularly your own! Enable everybody to have their say without feeling intimidated, put down, or embarrassed.
- Have a very clear idea of what you want each session to achieve.
- More is less! A good leader facilitates by developing the skill and aptitudes of everybody in the group.
- Learning is more effective when people do it for themselves.
- Make it fun!
- Ensure practical application. Ground the sessions in the reality of people's daily lives.
- Have a balance and diversity of activities. Think carefully about the balance of each session. Parts should be pacey and crisp, other parts should provide space for thinking and reflection.
- Be flexible. There is no need to stick rigidly to the notes – develop your own strategies and ideas, but do stick to the principles.
- Be sensitive to people.
- Encourage people to say how they feel, not just what they think.
- Genuinely listen to what is being said – don't interpret what is being said into your own experience and/or be thinking about what you are going to say back!
- When making a contribution yourself make it short, sharp, stimulating, and relevant to the session.
- Avoid polarisation and/or taking sides. Affirm every contribution. If

something is irrelevant or just plain wrong, do not correct! Ask intelligent questions of the group to get the session back on focus.
- Make sure everybody knows everybody else.
- Keep personal anecdotes to a minimum; if and when you use one, make sure it is relevant.
- Finish every session with a social time.
- Take an interest in group members, their work, family, hobbies, holidays, etc.

## Use of questions
- Don't answer every question which arises, but ask another one to set people thinking and discussing.
- Do not ask a question which assumes an answer.
- Never answer your own question.
- Encourage group members to pose questions, and remember that the only stupid question is the one you don't ask.

## Ready for next time
- Ground conclusions in the Bible.
- Talk regularly with people between meetings.
- Encourage reflection on what has been learned and get people to summarise.
- Pray about it.

## A point to ponder
As a relatively young teacher I was scheduled to have one of my lessons in school evaluated by a colleague. Knowing I was going to be observed teaching I prepared thoroughly! When it was time for the lesson I was firing on all cylinders. The class entered silently, sat passively, and I swung into action! During the next hour I used every means at my disposal to impress the class and my observing colleague.

Video was used, textbooks referred to, notes taken, and above all I spoke to the class with a passion and level of erudition that was nothing less than impressive! I was so good even I wanted to take notes! Not a sound was heard throughout the lesson and on the bell they stood and exited silently and respectfully.

What teaching! I could barely wait for the feedback to affirm what an outstanding lesson it had been. I was not disappointed, at least not initially. My observer confirmed that it had been outstanding teaching. Eloquent, relevant, interesting, dynamic, and focused, but then came the bit that mattered. It was one of the most telling and helpful observations ever given me as a teacher. 'Great teaching,' said the observer, 'but not a lot of learning. Always remember, a lesson has not been taught until it has been learned.'

In other words the students had been passive recipients and not active participants, and learning was nowhere near as effective as it should have been. Not such a great lesson after all!

It was the beginning of a stimulating, enriching, and challenging journey. I changed and developed so as to ensure that those for whom I had responsibility became active learners and not just the passive victims on the receiving end of what I felt they needed to know.

## In the beginning

When a group first forms or there is an influx of new members, it is a good exercise to contract together. Divide the group into smaller groups of 4/5 people and ask them to list the ground rules or contract they would like to work to, record them on a large sheet of paper and then after regrouping the whole group agree how they are going to work together. The type of ground rules might include items such as:

- Confidentiality. What is said in the group stays in the group.
- Start on time.
- Active listening.
- Mutual respect.
- Pray for one another.
- Share work and responsibilities.
- Support one another.
- No put downs.
- Regular social time together.

The contract could be neatly written out and every member given a copy, preferably credit card size and laminated to slip inside a wallet or handbag.

Another complementary strategy is to post in the room, at least for the first few meetings, a large copy of the ground rules. It is important that the group leader ensures that attention is drawn to the ground rules when appropriate. The best way is often to ask the question at a point of divergence, such as: 'Hold on . . . are we working within our ground rules at the moment?'

## How to ensure a thriving group

A healthy group will be characterised by the following:

- **Prayer**

  Everybody regularly prays for the group, both individually in private, and in the group meeting itself. If one member keeps a prayer log this is a good way of sustaining the focus on prayer. Write a brief summary of each prayer and date it. Check for answers every meeting.

- **Clarity**

  People know one another, they know what is happening, they know what is expected of them, they know the purpose of the group, and they know when and where the next meeting is taking place.

- **Quality**

  Everything is done properly, dare we say professionally. People are turned off by sloppiness. Committed preparation is undertaken by all taking part, particularly the leaders, resources are prepared well in advance and are to hand on the evening, questions are focused and well prepared.

- **Responsibility**

  Everybody shares responsibility for making the group a success, everybody is involved, and everybody is made to feel appreciated.

- **Rewards**

  Members feel the group is worthwhile, it is a rewarding experience to go. People are affirmed, thanked, and supported. They are made to feel that their contributions are appreciated and above all they are enriched by personal learning. Remember birthdays and celebrate special events together – it's a small gesture but much appreciated.

● **Pace**
Sessions do not 'drag', there is a healthy pace to the programme, people are stretched in a non-threatening fashion and genuine learning takes place.

# Structure of the sessions

Here's a guide as to the make-up of the sessions in this study series.

 ## Background notes

These are designed to help you feel confident in leading the session. It is helpful if you read them several times in preparation for the meeting. Deepening your personal knowledge will give you the confidence to lead and guide the group through the session. The notes can be used in a variety of ways:

▸ background reading to deepen your knowledge and understanding and/or any other group member leading a particular session

▸ enable you to formulate appropriate questions for the group to consider

▸ on some occasions you might think it appropriate to teach some of the material to the group

▸ the notes can be photocopied for group members, either as preparation for the meeting or for further study

▸ as a stimulus for further reading/study

 ## Resources

These lists briefly set out the resources you will need to lead the session. In some cases photocopiable materials are provided to be used as an icebreaker exercise or to support learning.

## Activities

The suggested activities are purely that – suggestions. The background notes may prompt you to add other questions, follow a different emphasis, and/or provide the stimulus for some teaching. These notes are not designed to be followed slavishly. They are like a list of ingredients in a recipe from which you can make an appropriate meal.

They are designed to engage participants actively in learning and to develop confidence and leadership/teaching skills in group members. Bear in mind that a person remembers:

▸ 10 per cent of what they hear
▸ 15 per cent of what they read
▸ 80 per cent of what they experience.

So use the notes within the context of the principles set out on page 5.

 ## Points to ponder

These are quotations designed to stimulate further thinking and discussion. They can be used in a variety of ways:

▸ Integrated into the programme.
▸ Reflection between sessions.
▸ Discussion starters.
▸ Further development of the ideas in a session.
▸ Stimulus for further reading and research.
▸ Prompts for praying.

## ( ) Closing prayer

A simple prayer is appended to the end of each session. They can be used in a variety of ways:

▸ To draw the session to a close.
▸ To initiate a time of prayer.
▸ To help particular participants develop confidence in praying aloud in the group.
▸ To stimulate discussion.

*Note*
There are two questionnaires at the back of the book. These are not designed to provide detailed statistical data, just a general indication of strengths and weaknesses to inform the future development of the group.

The first is designed for you, the leader, to complete in order to raise your awareness of your strengths and weaknesses. It is important that you are ruthlessly honest, and if you are really courageous and determined to improve, you could photocopy it, give it to at least some group members and ask them to complete it on you!

If this highlights significant issues they may well need talking through with somebody you trust and who can help and support you in developing your leadership skills. Good leaders are not born, they learn!

The second questionnaire is specifically designed for group members to complete and to provide leaders with some insight into how members are experiencing the group.

The distribution, collection and collation of the questionnaires is best done by somebody who does not lead the group but who can quickly provide a summary of the responses for the whole group to discuss. It could be completed by group members during the final session.

# Prayer

*But when you pray, do not be like the hypocrites, for they love to pray standing in the synagogues and on the street corners to be seen by men. I tell you the truth, they have received their reward in full. When you pray, go into your room, close the door and pray to your Father, who is unseen. Then your Father, who sees what is done in secret, will reward you. And when you pray, do not keep on babbling like pagans, for they think they will be heard because of their many words. Do not be like them, for your Father knows what you need before you ask him.*

**Matthew 6:5-8**

 ## Aims

At the end of the session people should:
▶ have a broader vision of what it means to pray
▶ have a deeper understanding of the Bible passage
▶ understand the structure of the Lord's Prayer
▶ be encouraged and/or challenged to develop their prayer life

 ## Background notes

The Jews in Jesus' day had set times for prayer and if people planned it right they could be in a very public place at the time of prayer, meet their obligation to pray *and* impress everybody! These prayers were frequently loud and theatrical, and often consisted of the mechanical repetition of set prayers.

By such performances some sought the approbation of their fellow men. They got it, but that is all they received! It can be hard to resist a little ostentatious spirituality, a little high-profile personal piety, but the enjoyment of public attention can be a real barrier to the development of our relationship with God. I attended a public carol service at which the preacher was more concerned with his public image than with getting the Christmas message across. He was tall, dark, handsome; wore all the latest pop fashion, insisted on walking about with a microphone stuck to his chin, waved his arms about in spectacular fashion, and generally cut a pretty impressive figure. Unfortunately he was so concerned with image he had not prepared thoroughly enough, kept prancing off away from his notes and forgetting what he wanted to say. He ended up delivering a weak, wandering, and generally unintelligible message! If we seek to impress people, that will be the sum total of our reward and the message of the Gospel will get lost as people's attention is on the performer rather than the message.

Prayer is not to be used as a means of impressing other people with our piety or of increasing our reputation as a godly person. Prayer is fundamentally a private activity between the individual and God, although that is not to say that there is not a place for public prayer. Public prayer should be a natural extension of our private prayer life, the tip of a prayer iceberg, and, as such, public prayer should be short and to the point, as opposed to the discursive conversation we may have with God in private.

I love the story of the little boy who was praying in his bedroom at the top of his voice for a train set for Christmas. His mother called out: 'James, pray quietly – God is not deaf!' To which James replied: 'I know, but Grandma is!' Jesus says we are to pray with an audience of one – God.

The word that is translated as *babble* is a very rare Greek word – *battalogeo* – which occurs nowhere else in the Bible or Greek literature. It is probably an onomatopoeic word based on a similar Greek word – *battarizo* – which means to stammer or stutter.

An amusing if somewhat speculative attempt has been made to suggest that *battalogeo* is based on the name of Battus; one person with that name was a king who stuttered, and the other a poet renowned for his verbosity and long-windedness!

The Gentiles, and in some cases the Jews, believed that their prayers would be heard and would be especially efficacious if they were long and repetitive. Basically it is immature and superficial to somehow think that the effectiveness of our prayers is in some way directly proportionate to the number of words we use, the eloquence of our phrasing, or the level of passion we inject into our intercessions.

When Elijah challenged the prophets of Baal on Mount Carmel, they resorted to long, loud, energetic, repetitive praying! Elijah mocks them with biting sarcasm, suggesting their gods may be meditating, or asleep, or just wandering off (1 Kings 18:20-40).

Either way this is a good example of how those without a deep personal relationship with God can assume their prayers will be heard.

Perhaps one of the most forthright and challenging statements about prayer comes at the end of the incident in which Jesus heals the young man suffering convulsions.

Jesus and three of the disciples ascend a mountain and there Jesus is transfigured before them. They see Jesus conversing with Moses and Elijah, and radiant with something of the glory of heaven. What a profound, exhilarating, mysterious, and overwhelmingly wonderful experience for them. One writer considers this incident as fundamental to our understanding of Jesus' ministry. The mount of transfiguration is the place where:

‣ The living and the dead are seen to be one in Christ;
‣ The old and new covenants are seen to be inseparable and complementary;
‣ The Cross and the glory are seen to go hand in hand;
‣ Human nature is seen to be destined for glory.

Whatever the deep theological significance of the Transfiguration may be, clearly placed as it is within the context of Jesus' teaching about his death, it would have been a profoundly encouraging experience for his disciples.

And yet almost immediately they return to the harsh realities of everyday life. In every sense of the word they came back down to earth with a bump.

In sharp contrast to the glory on the mountain is the scene of frustration and defeat that awaited Jesus and the three when they returned. They were immediately confronted with a demoniac boy and his father who passionately and poignantly spells out for Jesus what is wrong with his son:

‣ He is struck dumb;
‣ He throws himself around in an uncontrollable fashion;
‣ He foams at the mouth;
‣ He gnashes his teeth;
‣ He becomes rigid.

14

The ultimate frustration is the impotence of Jesus' disciples. Despite their best efforts they have made no impact on the situation! Without more ado Jesus heals the boy. All are astonished, none more so than the disciples. 'Why could we not heal the boy?' is their urgent question.

Jesus reply is staggering. All they need is a little faith. Then all things become possible. In these situations you must also add in a strong element of prayer and fasting. Jesus is challenging them to get serious with God (Matthew 17:1-22, Mark 9:2-29, Luke 9:28-43).

The power and authority of Jesus so clearly displayed on the mountain to Peter, James and John is here seen in action in the healing of the young man. This same power and authority is available to us through faith and prayer.

In 2 Chronicles 20 we read of Jehoshaphat, king of Judah, being confronted with an overwhelmingly superior hostile army. Although fear strikes deep into his heart, he does not lose his eternal perspective. We read that he sets himself to seek the Lord and then he proclaims a fast throughout the whole of Judah. The people gather before God and fast and pray. 'We do not know what to do, but our eyes are on you,' is their cry. Jehoshaphat's position is clear – it is that if they believe in God they will be established. And so it is. By faith, prayer and fasting the people are delivered!

We need to be resolute in our praying. To set ourselves to seek the Lord in a rigorous and disciplined fashion.

Some years ago my younger son Simon and a friend sailed a 40-foot catamaran back to England from southern Ireland in a force nine gale. I asked him how he did it. Simply, they stood in the cockpit of the yacht for three days without sleep, food, or drink, and resolutely sailed it to England.

No matter how strong the wind, how high the waves, how tired and hungry they became, they were not going to be deflected from their task. After three days they sailed safely into Plymouth. Their strength, resolution, and dedication had brought success. So it should be in our prayer lives. Our prayers need to be focused, resolute, and determined.

**The overall structure of the prayer**

Jesus is giving us a model prayer, which can be prayed as it is, but also indicates the appropriate structure and content for our own praying. People use the Lord's Prayer in a number of ways:

> ‣ Just by praying it as it is;

▸ Using each phrase as a starter to gently expand their praying into the territory indicated by the phrase;

▸ As a blueprint to encompass the widest possible repertoire of praying.

The first three petitions focus on the future consummation of the kingdom of God, yet with present implications for the manner in which we lead our lives. The second three focus on our present needs. By virtue of their order it is clear that concern for the kingdom of God takes precedence over individual personal needs, reflecting the saying of Jesus: 'Seek first the kingdom of God . . .' so that one's personal needs must always be seen within the context of the kingdom of God.

*The first three petitions focus on:*
God's name;
God's kingdom;
God's will.
    *'On earth as in heaven.'*

*The second three petitions focus on:*
Our physical needs;
Our need for forgiveness;
Our need for spiritual protection and victory.

*Another way of looking at the prayer is to regard it as having five elements:*
Worship of the Father;
The kingdom of the Father;
Provision by the Father;
The grace of the Father;
The protection of the Father.

Whichever way we look at the Lord's Prayer it is remarkable for its conciseness, clarity, and spiritual depth. It contains few words, but those words have great profundity.

 ## Resources

▸ Photocopy the boxes on pages 18-23 and paste on cards
▸ Paper, pens/pencils
▸ Flipchart and felt tips

## Activities

1　Ask everybody to write on a piece of A4 paper a brief definition of 'prayer'. Use felt tip markers and make the writing large enough to be read from a distance of about six feet. Ask people to put their definitions on the floor in the middle of the room. Extrapolate all the key words which help us to understand what prayer is. Write them up on a flipchart for all to see.

2　Brainstorm: How many different types of prayer are there?

3　Give out cards with the passages on and get people to read their passage. Identify the prayer principles established in each passage. If you have a big group you can split into two or three smaller groups, all do the same exercise and then compare conclusions.

4　If your group is up for it get them to write on a piece of paper (anonymously), the number of minutes they spend in prayer each day. Put all the numbers in the middle, average out the figures. Invite comments – too little prayer? If so, why? Discussion about the barriers / difficulties in praying. Any tips for successful praying?

5　Read the passage from Matthew 6 at the beginning of this chapter. An exercise to draw out the main points can again be done in small groups. Agree a headline for the passage. Agree the three or four main points. Identify the key points for a full understanding of the passage. This hierarchy of information aids learning. Identify the prayer principles established in this passage.

HEADLINE

THREE OR FOUR MAIN POINTS

DETAIL WHICH ADDS TO OUR UNDERSTANDING

6　Can we all commit to pray for a few minutes every day between now and when we next meet? Agree some things to pray for.

**Different aspects of prayer**
Use the photocopies of the boxes on the following pages, pasted on card. Use as many as you wish. Try to give each person in the group at least one card, preferably a week before the meeting.

At the meeting each person takes it in turn to read the passage, followed by a discussion to identify the fundamental teaching about prayer contained in each passage. The brief notes are designed to help the group member start and guide the discussion.

These sections are not meant to be an exhaustive list of the scripture's teaching on prayer. There may well be other sections of scripture you prefer to use.

Invite members of the group to share other portions of the scripture that they have found helpful, challenging, or just plain puzzling.

---

### I Thessalonians 5:16-18
*Message*: Pray cheerfully and continually

Paul, in writing to the Thessalonians, sets out a liturgy of spirituality in chapter 5. Here he grounds prayer in God's will for his people. To pray is to manifest God's will in our lives and there are three characteristics set out here:

▶ rejoice all the time;
▶ pray all the time;
▶ give thanks all the time.

We may be struggling, we may be in difficult circumstances, we may feel weak and helpless, but God gives us inner resources to rejoice and give thanks.

Just by being obedient to these two injunctions our mindset will change and we will see things from an eternal perspective. To pray continually means that every activity must be carried out in a spirit of prayerfulness, our whole lives should be pervaded with prayer, and we recognise that we live out our lives continually in the presence of God.

What does it mean for us to pray continually?

### John 16:23-24
*Message*: Pray boldly and confidently

The disciples of Jesus found it very difficult coming to terms with the idea of Jesus' death. For them much of his teaching was obscure and ambiguous and they were undoubtedly confused, not just intellectually, but emotionally.

But Jesus says it will not always be so – they will come to understand in the light of the Easter events and then when the Holy Spirit is given to them. In that day, profundity will be complemented by simplicity. Nowhere more so than in prayer.

Prayer is the deepest and most profound of spiritual activities, and yet the simplest. We ask, we receive, and we are filled with joy. Is this your experience?

### 2 Corinthians 1:10b-11
*Message*: Pray for others

Asking is a fundamental aspect of prayer and interceding on behalf of others is the backbone of that asking. Paul begins 2 Corinthians by telling them of the afflictions he and his colleagues experienced in Asia. They almost did not survive, but the fact that they did was in no small part due to the prayers of the Corinthians. Paul uses a strong Greek word to describe their praying – *sunupourgeo*, which literally means 'working together to support me'. Prayer is seen as hard work! For a long time there was a degree of conflict between Paul and the Corinthians.

Perhaps their praying for each other brought about a change of heart and mind.

How do our prayers affect the way we think and feel?

**Romans 15:30-33**

*Message:* Pray for strugglers

Just as Corinthians was written with passion fired up by strong emotions, Romans is Paul's reflective letter. The Corinthians are thanked for their passionate praying, the Christians in Rome are urged to pray for Paul as he struggles to make the Gospel known and faces opposition as he does so.

Things may be going fairly smoothly for us, nevertheless, we can share in the struggles of others by praying for them and with them. We pray for their deliverance, their victory, and that they may be joyful and refreshed.

Who particularly needs our prayers at the moment?

**Ephesians 6:10-12**

*Message:* Engage the enemy

Paul reminds the Ephesians that the difficulties they face, the trials they experience, the barriers they have to overcome, are spiritual rather than temporal.

We may live in the world but our responsibility is to demolish the enemy's empire. When we pray we engage with those spiritual forces and as such will need all the help we can get.

This is why prayer is so important. It is the realm in which we engage directly with the enemy. He will do all in his power to keep us from prayer. 2 Corinthians 10:3-5 is an eloquent commentary on this warfare.

Can we think of any areas in which the church is engaged in this spiritual warfare?

**Exodus 17:8-13**
*Message*: Keep praying!

The Israelites have escaped from Egypt. Led by Moses they are in the wilderness on their way to the Promised Land. They are struggling from one crisis to another and now they are attacked by the Amalekites, the descendants of Esau.

This is a vivid portrayal of what it means to persevere in prayer. Even when tired, Moses continues to hold up his hands to God, assisted by his brother. This is an incident full of characters but central to all that happens is God. Once more he delivers his people as they pray. At the end of the story Moses erects an altar to Yahweh and calls it 'The Lord is my banner'.

How can we support one another in persistent praying?

**I Kings 3:5-10**
*Message*: Pray for wisdom

God comes to Solomon in a dream and asks what he should give him. Solomon asks for a discerning heart and an understanding mind in order that he should know the difference between good and evil and be able to work out this discernment in the governance of his people.

God answers his prayer and Solomon has come to epitomise wisdom ever since. The word heart in Hebrew means the whole person – emotions, intellect, will, desires. Solomon prays that God will permeate every aspect of his being and that he will be able to live his life powered by God's gifting.

If God were to ask us the question: 'What shall I give you?' what would be our prayer?

## James 5:13-16
*Message:* Prayer works!

This is one of the most powerful passages on prayer in the New Testament. In trying circumstances we do not adopt a passive, stoical stance and neither do we get hot under the collar and storm around trying to sort things out aggressively. We pray, we praise, and if we are sick, we get others to pray with us and for us.

Prayers do not necessarily change our circumstances – God is not some divine slot machine automatically dispensing what we think we need. But prayer does provide strength, resilience, and puts things back into perspective. We see things with God's eyes, not just our own, and remind ourselves that prayer must be seen within the context of God's love, sovereignty and providence.

What are the practical implications of this passage for your group and for your church?

## 2 Kings 19:8-15
*Message:* When in trouble . . . pray!

I love this story. Hezekiah is a godly man and a good king. But being the king of a small, strategically placed nation, surrounded by the big boys of Egypt and Assyria, meant he was under a lot of diplomatic, military, and political pressure. Sennacherib, the Assyrian king, describes having shut up Hezekiah in Jerusalem like a bird in a cage! The threats come thick and fast. Hezekiah knows that no amount of administrative or political manoeuvring is going to avail with Sennacherib. He turns to prayer and in so doing regains his perspective and sees the situation as it really is – that is, he sees it as God sees it.

Have you ever been under intense pressure, prayed, and found God really does undertake?

## Colossians 4:12-13
*Message*: Work at it

Epaphras is one of those New Testament saints we know little about. A native of Colossae where he was an evangelist, also an evangelist to Laodicea and Hieropolis. Colossae faced an influx of false teaching and Epaphras' response was to pray and work hard to counter the false teaching.

Prayer and hard work go together. Epaphras wrestling in prayer reminds us of Jacob who wrestled with the angel and would not let go until he was blessed. We may not always feel like praying, that is the time to pray! Then we complement our prayers by working hard to build God's kingdom. Personal piety has a practical dimension.

How are we building on our prayers by working for God's kingdom?

## Luke 18:1-5
*Message*: Persevere in prayer

The judge in this story is a crook. He is exactly what a judge should not be. Jesus is probably referring to the judges appointed by Herod or the Romans. Officially they were called Dayyaneh Gezeroth – judges of punishment – but locally on the ground they were called Dayyaneh Gezeloth – robber judges.

The widow had no chance – she was not wealthy or well connected, yet by her sheer persistence she embarrasses the judge into awarding in her favour.

There is a wonderful phrase in the Greek which is translated along the lines, 'keeps bothering me', but it can also mean to give somebody a black eye!

The whole point of the story is to contrast the judge with our heavenly Father.

What are the barriers to our persevering in prayer and how do we overcome them?

**Points to ponder**

> ▸ *Character is what you do in the dark.* **Dwight L. Moody**

> ▸ *On my bed I remember you;*
> *I think of you through the watches of the night.*
> *Because you are my help,*
> *I sing in the shadow of your wings.*
> *I stay close to you;*
> *your right hand upholds me.* **Psalm 63:6-8**

> ▸ Satan laughs at our words, mocks our toil, but trembles when we pray.

> ▸ What a man is on his knees before God, that he is and no more.

> ▸ Prayer is not the means of us getting more of God, but the means for God to get more of us.

> ▸ The brevity of the Lord's Prayer could be because it concentrates on just a few fundamental truths. In our day and age we go around with too much excess baggage in our lives and need to recapture the beautiful simplicity encapsulated in this prayer.

> ▸ *The Lord's Prayer contains the sum total of religion and morals.* **The Duke of Wellington**

> ▸ Prayer is the vehicle whereby we subordinate our lives to God.

> ▸ *Everything we do in the Christian life is easier than prayer.* **Dr Martin Lloyd Jones**

## ( ) **Closing prayer**

*Heavenly Father,*
We thank you for the gift of prayer.
We thank you that you hear and answer our prayers.
The answer may not always be as we would have wished, but you only ever do what is good and right for us. Thank you.
We confess that our praying is so often poor and feeble. We are deeply conscious of our need to pray more and to this end we ask that you anoint us with your Holy Sprit.
Teach us to pray thoughtfully, intelligently, and creatively.
Teach us to pray with passion and perseverance.
Teach us to stand together and pray boldly.
Enable us to hear your voice and to be open to your leading and guiding.
Help us to be sensitive to the needs of others, and to love and support one another in our praying.
And like Solomon we pray for wisdom to discern the difference between good and evil, and to have the strength and grace always to choose the good in all we think, say and do.
Through Jesus Christ our Lord,
*Amen*

## Personal notes relating to session one | Key Bible verses

# Our Father

*Our Father in heaven, hallowed be your name . . .*
**Matthew 6:9b**

 **Aims**

At the end of the session people should:
> have a deeper appreciation of the concept of God as Father
> have a deeper understanding of some of the names of God
> have a deeper understanding of what it means 'to hallow' God's name in their lives
> have actively participated in either session one or session two

 **Background notes**

The Greeks believed in many gods. They were capricious, unpredictable, hostile, unpleasant, and generally to be avoided! People lived in a constant state of apprehension that they had failed to undertake the appropriate religious ritual to keep the gods happy and content. How liberating now to find there is but one God and he is a Father, and that we need no longer cower before the hordes of arbitrary and changeable deities but rest in the father heart of God. Jesus firmly puts God as Father centre stage of his teaching about the nature and character of God.

**'Our Father . . .'** Suggests two things:
i) **Intimacy**
God is our Father. This was a radically new interpretation of our relationship with God, a distinctive perspective. The Jews saw God as

Lord, and emphasised his transcendence, the awe in which we should hold him, his holiness – none of which are wrong, but they did not see God as Father. The notion of God as transcendent is still in this prayer – he is 'Our Father, who art in heaven' – and yet the prayer begins with this sense of a filial relationship with the creator of the universe.

ii) **Corporateness**

God is not my Father but our Father, reminding us that the Christian faith is fundamentally a family affair. We belong to a worshipping and praying community – Christianity is not a faith that can be lived in splendid isolation. We work out the implications and responsibilities of our relationship with God in our relationships within the church.

Although the concept of God as Father is not unknown in the Old Testament it is not the dominant image for God. In the Old Testament the lordship of God is emphasised with strong moral and ethical overtones. Any sense that we are God's children emphasises the need for us to emulate him in our commitment to truth and justice. The Old Testament image of God as Father is primarily one of filial obedience and strength of character. Jesus' emphasis on God as Father brings to the Old Testament concept a strong emotional dimension. God is now Abba, an Aramaic word best translated as something between father and daddy. Jesus alone uses this intimate word and in so doing effectively redefines the nature of our relationship with God.

There is a warmth and intimacy which complements the sterner dimension of the Fatherhood of God as revealed in the Old Testament. We are adopted sons and daughters with all that implies for commitment and obedience, complemented by the love of the Father for his children. This loving relationship between father and child has a number of characteristics:

- ▶ Mutual trust;
- ▶ A father is somebody there when you need them most;
- ▶ A father cultivates a sense of confidence and security in their child;
- ▶ A father ensures adequate provision for his children;
- ▶ The relationship is one to be enjoyed rather than endured;

> ‣ A caring father disciplines his children;
> ‣ The father provides an excellent role model and the child learns from the father.

Some years ago a man attempted to get into the White House to see the president of the United States. He wanted to bring to the president's attention a matter of great concern to him. Needless to say he did not get very far. On a dozen occasions he was turned back from the main gate by the guards stationed there. Eventually he sat on the kerb and buried his head in his hands, defeated, frustrated, and in the depths of despair.

After a while he was approached by a small boy who asked him why he was in such a state. The man explained how he had hoped to see the president but could not get anywhere near him. His wish was thwarted at the first hurdle, the guard on the gate. The young boy said: 'Come with me.' Together they approached the White House gate and passed through unchallenged. Across the grounds, through the West Wing, right into the Oval Office. Not once were they challenged, stopped, accosted, or prevented from entering the presence of the president. The man was dumbfounded. As they entered the Oval Office the president looked at the boy and said, 'Hi! What can I do for you two?' The boy replied: 'Dad, I would like you to listen to this man.'

**'Hallowed be your name . . .'**

The name of a person and their personality/characteristics were inextricably bound together in Jewish thought. To honour the name is to honour the person. We pray here that God will be treated with high regard, both a prayer for the future when his kingdom will be finally established on earth, but a prayer for the present, that God's name will be honoured in our lives and in our community.

The phrase is potent with meaning. God's name is hallowed through his people acting righteously; we are called to be holy, to be separate from the world and its standards. Thereby we communicate to the world the holiness or hallowedness of God.

Ezekiel communicates the same message in chapter 36:22f. where he describes the return of the exiles to Jerusalem as something accomplished by God so that God's name is no longer taken lightly among the nations. God acts to restore the honour of his name.

God is the one who saves, restores, and establishes righteousness.

In her book *Amazing Grace*, Kathleen Norris writes about people who reflect the image of God presented in the Bible. They say: 'I just can't handle it!'

Whilst appreciating the undoubted genuineness of such people, she challenges the notion of a God we can handle, by saying: 'If we seek a God we can "handle", that will be exactly what we get. A God we can manipulate, suspiciously like ourselves, the wideness of whose mercy we've cut down to size.'

 ## Resources

- ▸ Copies of page 35
- ▸ Copies of the verses noted on page 32 for people to read and discuss, or you may wish to use Bibles
- ▸ Post-it notes
- ▸ Paper
- ▸ Blu-Tack

 ## Activities

1 Pick up where you left off last week. How have people been doing in their praying? Has it made a difference? What have been the difficulties? What has helped? What has hindered? (You could prime a couple of people to get you started.) Opportunity for a bit more discussion of the difficulties/ barriers, with some suggestions how to deal with them.

2 Circulate copies of page 35. Ask people to read it through quietly, and then in small groups construct one sentence to sum up what this passage is saying. Get the groups to write

out the sentence on a large sheet of paper, pin them up and give people the opportunity to wander round and have a look.

3   Refer to the passage Matthew 6:9b – what do you remember most about your father? What characteristics did you most appreciate? This is potentially sensitive territory. Keep it purely voluntary and comfortable, with no long silences!

4   Brainstorm – what are the attributes of a good father? Do they tell us anything about God?

5   Are there any motherly attributes to God? Refer to:
   ▸ Isaiah 49:14-15
   ▸ Isaiah 66:13
   ▸ Deuteronomy 32:18
   ▸ Matthew 23:37

   How do these verses add to our understanding of God?

   *Note*: These gender issues are useful but limited in the sense that any language, metaphor, or simile used in helping us to understand God is of limited value, but we should not shy away from the fact that the Bible refers to God as Father. The Fatherhood of God cannot be totally defined in terms of our experience of our earthly father. Such experience generates helpful insights but is not definitive. The defining relationship is that between Jesus and his Father. 'We must transcend human categories in general, and gender categories in particular.'

6   What does hallowed mean? How do we do it?

7   Finally we will look at some of the names of God. Find out the meaning of the names of the people in your group. Put names and meanings on separate Post-it notes, one colour for names and another for meanings, and get people to match them up. You could add names/meanings of people in the church to make it more fun! Then match the names of God with their meanings in the same way, either by photocopying the sheet or using Post-it notes.

8 Finish with a time of prayer, asking for a deeper personal and corporate experience of God in his various names. Use the prayer on page 34 either to start or end the time of prayer.

| Names/Titles of God in the Old Testament | Meaning | Reference |
|---|---|---|
| Yahweh | *I am what I am* | Exodus 3:14 |
| El Elyon | *God Most High* | Genesis 14:18-20 |
| El Roi | *God of seeing* | Genesis 16:13 |
| El Olam | *The Everlasting God* | Genesis 21:33 |
| El Shaddai | *God Almighty* | Genesis 17:1 |
| El Berith | *God of the Covenant* | Judges 9:46 |
| Yahweh Sabaoth | *Lord of hosts* | 2 Samuel 5:10 |
| Melek | *King* | Psalm 24:7-10 |
| El Elohe Israel | *God the God of Israel* | Genesis 33:20 |

For the people of the Bible names were full of meaning. The name of a person or place or god was intimately connected with their personality, status, or nature. If your status or nature changed, so too could your name. For example:

> Abram became Abraham (Genesis 17:1-8)
> Jacob became Israel (Genesis 32:22-32)
> Mattaniah became Zedekiah (2 Kings 24:17)

Can you think of any others?

 ## Points to ponder

> The whole miracle of saving grace is summed up in the one word – Father.

> *He that has seen me has seen the Father.* **Jesus**

>       *Restore O Lord,*
>       *the honour of your Name!*
>       *In works of sovereign power*
>       *come shake the earth again,*
>       *that men may see,*
>       *and come with reverent fear,*
>       *to the Living God,*
>       *whose Kingdom shall outlast the years.*
>       **Graham Kendrick and Chris Rolinson**

Restore O Lord by Graham Kendrick and Chris Rolinson. Copyright © 1981 Thankyou Music/Adm. by worshiptogether.com songs excl. UK & Europe, adm. by Kingsway Music, tym@kingsway.co.uk, used by persmission.

> Whatever may happen to you, and whatever your circumstances, God is your Father. As such he loves you, takes an active interest in you, and is committed to your welfare. As Father he can do no other.

> God's cheques never bounce.

# ⟨⟩ Closing prayer

*Dear Heavenly Father,*
Thank you for your love for me.
Thank you that through Christ we are adopted into your family, we become your sons and daughters.
Thank you for all those times when we have been particularly aware of your Father's love for us.
Thank you that you never fail, you never let us down, you are the same 'yesterday, today, and forever'.
I acknowledge the weakness and frailty of my love for you and pray that you will give me a fresh vision of what it means to be your child.
Kindle deeper love and devotion in my heart and empower me to work out my relationship with you in my daily life.
May my life glorify your Name.
Through Jesus Christ our Lord.
*Amen*

## Resource

You can sum up the whole teaching of the New Testament in one phrase. 'Our Father . . .'

Immortal God, the Creator and sustainer of the universe, is revealed to us as Abba, 'Father'.

A Christian's spirituality could be defined by the extent to which they are aware of God as Father and the practical impact that awarenesss makes upon the way they live their lives.

If a Christian does not have a sound grasp of the concept of God as Father and if that reality is not the driving force of their life, it could be said that they do not have a genuine understanding of what it means to be a Christian.

| Personal notes relating to session two | Key Bible verses |
| --- | --- |
|  |  |

# Your kingdom come

*. . . your kingdom come, your will be done on earth as it is in heaven.*

**Matthew 6:10**

 **Aims**

At the end of this session people should:

> ‣ have a deeper understanding of the kingdom of God
> ‣ have a deeper appreciation of the practical outworking of God's kingdom
> ‣ commit to practical involvement in extending the kingdom of God
> ‣ know what is expected of them for the next session

 **Background notes**

This petition is the practical outworking of the previous one. To 'hallow' the name of God is to be committed and obedient in order to extend his kingdom. We move from God as Father to God as King, thereby avoiding any notion of superficiality or sentimentality in the idea of God as Father.

The Jews who heard Jesus would have been impressed and excited by talk of the kingdom of God. After generations of subservience to successive empires, they were longing for a Messiah (the anointed one), leading them to throw off the oppressive Roman regime and establish a dominant Israel. Jewish messianic hope was strongly militaristic. No wonder that when Jesus said to his disciples: 'Follow me!', they did. It took the disciples a long while to understand that Jesus' kingdom was not a socio-political one. This accounts for the fact that when Jesus was arrested Peter was quick to pick up his sword. He thought it was time for the Messiah to fight!

Instead of which Jesus presents a radical paradigm shift. It was this shift of understanding which constantly astounded his hearers. Jesus depoliticised the concept of the kingdom. For him it is a question of personal commitment, grounded in faith, rather than an accident of birth. No longer is the kingdom to be identified with the nation of Israel but with all who respond to him in personal faith and commitment.

Jesus was not offering liberation from Roman rule or the restoration of Israel's political power, but emancipation from those spiritual powers which bind the heart and mind. Followers of Jesus are called to a new spiritual life which is characterised by a new ethical ideal.

This shift from a militarist understanding to a greatly enhanced ethical understanding echoed the position of the great Old Testament prophets. Nowhere is this ethical dimension seen more clearly and forcefully than in the Sermon on the Mount.

The ethical teaching of the kingdom is enshrined in the Sermon on the Mount, and yet this is not a new law, a new set of do's and don'ts, but a powerful expression of what the new kingdom of God is to be like. When we pray: 'Thy kingdom come', this is what we are praying for. The Sermon on the Mount is not a legalistic requirement but a natural expression of our new kingdom life. As such the teaching is not a heavy burden to be borne, but a new way of living to be embraced. The Sermon is the practical expression of the Kingdom of God, a kingdom completely different from the one we live in. It is no accident that the Lord's Prayer comes right in the middle of the Sermon on the Mount.

Any study series such as this is likely to spark discussion in the group centred on the question: 'How does this relate to modern life?' So, for example, the action taken by the US-led coalition in Iraq in 2003 could be a talking point. Men, women, and children were killed, ostensibly to preserve our way of life in the face of terrorist threats. Some people might ask how this action is in line with the Sermon on the Mount?

> ▸ 'Blessed are the peacemakers . . .'
> ▸ 'You are the salt of the earth . . .'
> ▸ 'Do not resist the evildoer . . .'
> ▸ 'Love your enemies and pray for those who persecute you . . .'

When these questions arise it is to be hoped that your group will not want to adopt a simplistic 'head in the sand' approach but instead make a genuine attempt to interpret contemporary political and socio-economic realities in the light of the teaching of Jesus.

Christians have a radically different agenda from that of kings, dictators, presidents, and politicians. Our task is to extend the kingdom of righteousness and the Sermon on the Mount gives us an indication of how we can do that. But it must be done in the power of God's Spirit and not by our own legalistically driven efforts.

In Jesus' day it was the scribes and Pharisees who followed the path of rigorous legalistic morality. They were not inherently bad people. They were men of conviction and devotion. They were in many ways devout and moral, held in high regard by the people, but they lacked a genuine experience of God's Spirit in their lives and so their good works became dead works. When faced with the reality of God's Spirit in Jesus they retrenched and opposed what they perceived to be a move away from their own carefully guarded rules and regulations. Is there a danger of the church stifling the Spirit of God by clinging to its own entrenched positions?

The radicality of this teaching is reinforced by the toughness of the requirements. There is no room for compromise with evil. There is no question of a middle way, of a mutual beneficial settlement with sin. 'The heart remains pure by making no concessions.' Jesus always challenges us to say 'yes' or 'no' – never 'maybe' or 'I'll think about it!'

The present reality of the kingdom is not only evident in the teaching of Jesus but also in his actions. The kingdom is here now, evidenced by the healing of the sick, the giving of sight to the blind, the fact that the lame are walking, and that good news is preached to the poor (Matthew 11:5).

At the same time there will be a future moment when the kingdom will be consummated by the return of Jesus. The New Testament writers also looked forward to the day when Jesus would return and inaugurate fully God's cosmic rule: 1 Corinthians 16:22; 2 Peter 3:13, Revelation 22:20.

Our responsibility is to work for the extension of the present kingdom and prepare ourselves for the return of Jesus. This future hope is also part of our present reality. Whenever the will of God is fulfilled in a person's life, his kingdom is extended. To pray for God's kingdom to come is to commit to a life of faith and obedience.

The kingdom of God is not a geographical location, but it is located in the hearts and lives of those who love and obey him. God's rule is not geopolitical. It is in the hearts and lives of his disciples.

The kingdom of God is a major theme in Matthew's gospel and it is presented as something which is in the future *and* a present reality. The gospel is the good news that God's kingdom has come and been established on earth through the life, death, and resurrection of Jesus. This prayer is a prayer of commitment to that kingdom.

*So the sum of this supplication is that God will illuminate the heart by the light of his word, bring our hearts to obey his righteousness by the breathing of his Spirit, and restore to order at his will, all that is lying waste upon the face of the earth.* **John Calvin**

This petition has two dimensions:

1. A desire to see the consummation of God's kingdom as it now stands by the return of Jesus. Beautifully and powerfully described in Revelation 21:9-22:5.

2. A commitment to currently building the kingdom of God by our work and witness as outlined in Matthew 6:33.

This simple, straightforward phrase: 'Your kingdom come', challenges Christians to adopt a personal agenda radically different from that of the world. It will mean a radical reordering of our priorities. It will mean such things as:

- simplifying our lifestyles
- buying Fair Trade goods from supermarkets
- campaigning for justice
- giving money to the poor
- witnessing to our neighbours
- evangelising the community in which our church is situated
- using our church buildings and resources on behalf of the community
- changing our priorities
- challenging politicians

If we pray this prayer and mean it, we will change our lives.

 **Resources**

- Flipchart, pens, and Blu-Tack
- Video, if using a tape

 **Activities**

1    Brainstorm the words that you associate with 'kingdom'.
2    From all the words generated by the brainstorm, agree the five or six most important ones to be filtered out.
3    What are the practical implications for us of these five or six words?
4    Invite somebody to speak to the group who is at the cutting edge of extending God's kingdom. Interview them about their work, why they do it, what they hope to achieve, the problems they encounter, their strategies for success, etc.

     Suggestions:
     - A local Youth For Christ worker

> ▸ Somebody in a church plant

> ▸ A representative for TEARFund, Oxfam, Christian Aid, or Amnesty International

> ▸ A local minister and/or youth worker

> ▸ A representative from the local YMCA

> ▸ An RE teacher, Christian police officer or Christian social worker

An alternative is to show a video of radical Christianity in action, e.g. a *Transformations* video or a video from one of the charities.

5   What can we do as a group? Take on a practical commitment such as:

> ▸ 'Adopt' an overseas child and sponsor them with a regular collection at each meeting

> ▸ Regular giving to Christian Aid or TEARFund

> ▸ Consider regularly contacting local MP on issues of crucial importance

> ▸ Regularly support Amnesty International campaigns for prisoners of conscience

6   What are the issues currently in the news we ought to pray about?

Preparation for next meeting – allocate prayers/readings for Communion at the next meeting, see pages 47-48.

## Points to ponder

▶ Commitment is doing what you said you would do, when the mood in which you said it is passed.
▶ How is the kingdom of God synonymous with 'the Church'?
▶ Watch and pray.
▶ Let go and let God.
▶ *Those who pray for a better way of life in this generation must be willing to be part of God's solution.* **Warner**
▶ *Wherever the bounds of beauty, truth and goodness are advanced there the Kingdom comes.* **Donald Coggan**
▶ *The Kingdom of God is a kingdom of love; and love is never a stagnant pool.* **Henry du Bose**
▶ To pray 'Thy kingdom come,' is to pray 'My kingdom go'.

## ( ) Closing prayer

*Father,*
I have prayed many times for your kingdom to come, perhaps without realising the full implications of that prayer. Forgive me for not having worked harder at making your kingdom a reality in my life.
Give me wisdom and perception on how best to let you rule in me. May your Spirit guide and direct every aspect of my life: my thinking, my speaking and my behaving.
Enable me to work out my relationship with you in every area of my life; my home and family, my work, and in the church. May all I do bring glory to your Name and extend your kingdom.
Through Jesus Christ our Lord.
*Amen*

## Personal notes relating to session three | Key Bible verses

# Give us today

*Give us today our daily bread.*
**Matthew 6:11**

 ## Aims

At the end of the session people should:
- have a deeper appreciation of God's provision in every aspect of their lives
- commit to pray for the needs of at least one other group member for the next week

 ## Background notes

Here in the second half of the prayer the focus shifts to the needs of the disciples. In this case the very down-to-earth need of daily provision. The perspective changes from the cosmic dimension to the very ordinary reality of our daily lives.

And yet the very concept of bread, while being very basic to our daily lives, also has a spiritual/cosmic dimension – Jesus said: 'I am the bread of life.' In teaching us to pray the Lord's Prayer Jesus is deliberately inviting us to share in these ambiguities, the healthy tension between the eternal kingdom of God and the reality of life on earth.

The disciples of Jesus lived a pretty precarious existence, as do many Christians in the developing world today. Jesus makes it clear that his followers can trust the Father for practical daily provision. But these needs are just that – needs as opposed to wants. It is easy to get prayer wrong as did a certain John Ward, MP, who many years ago owned part of Dagenham:

*'O Lord, Thou knowest I have mine estates in the city of London, and likewise that I have lately purchased an estate in fee-simple in the County of Essex. I beseech Thee to preserve the two counties of Middlesex and Essex from fire and earthquake, and, as I have a mortgage in Hertfordshire, I beg of Thee likewise to have an eye of compassion on that county; for the rest of the counties, Thou mayest deal with them as Thou art pleased.'*

The word translated daily – *epiousios* – is quite an unusual word and can be translated 'daily' or it can be a word indicating measure rather than time, in which case the prayer is a prayer for the bread we need (in amount). 'Give us today the amount of bread we need.' Either interpretation indicates a fundamental dependence upon God for our daily needs.

The early church found difficulty in coming to terms with the notion that God was interested in our daily needs, and they tended to spiritualise this prayer by referring it to Communion and/or Jesus as the bread of life. Yet God is deeply concerned about our daily needs and we are to share with God what they are, emphasising our dependency upon him.

In a very profound way this petition links two aspects of our Christian lives:
- Daily dependence upon God
- Individual and corporate worship in the taking of Communion.

Just as there are three dimensions to the kingdom of God:
- Past – inaugurated by Jesus
- Present – working out in our lives and the life of the Church
- Future – consummation when Jesus comes again;

so there are three dimensions to Communion:
- Past – remembering the death of Jesus
- Present – a means of grace whereby we share his resurrection life
- Future – Jesus is coming again!

This simple meal of bread and wine is truly the meal of the kingdom.

**Resources**

- Candles and matches
- Photocopy of the story from Exodus on pages 50-51, cut and jumbled
- Bread and wine for Communion
- Photocopies of the news items on page 51 for next meeting

Before the meeting you will need to prepare Communion and to ask people to take on the various readings and prayers.

 **Activities**

1   Provide the group(s) with the story of the manna in the wilderness from Exodus 16, but cut it up and ask them to sort the sections into the correct order.
2   What do we learn about God from this passage?
3   What does daily bread mean for us who have Sainsbury's and Tesco?
4   Get each person to write on a piece of card a practical need they have. This can be done anonymously. Put all the cards in a pile, shuffle them, and get each person to take one and commit to pray for that need for the next week.
5   What did Jesus mean when he said: 'I am the bread of life'?
6   Prayer time and thanksgiving, leading into communion:
7   Communion:
    - Person A:    specific prayer for Communion
    - Person B:    read 1 Corinthians 11:23-24
    - Person C:    break the bread and pass it round
    - Person D:    read 1 Corinthians 11:25-26
    - Person E:    pass the cup round
    - Person F:    lead in the Lord's Prayer
    - Person G:    give each person a candle:

Light one person's candle. That person then prays, silently or aloud, for somebody across the room. When they have finished their prayer they get up and light that person's candle, who then prays for somebody else, and so on until all the candles are lit. Then everybody stands and together you pray the Lord's Prayer.

8    Lead into a simple fellowship supper of bread, cheese, biscuits and coffee/tea.

Preparation for next meeting:
Distribute the newspaper articles on page 51 for the next meeting and ask each person to underline what is for them the most striking phrase or sentence in each piece. At the next meeting they will be asked to read what they have underlined and say why they have done so.

 **Points to ponder**

> ▸ C. S. Lewis suggests that we may sometimes be reluctant to bring our small prayers to God because of our own sense of dignity and self-importance, rather than the dignity and importance of God.

> ▸ The degree of love in our hearts for other people is a barometer as to the level of our love for God.

> ▸ God is not unaware of our needs, nevertheless, asking is fundamental because we need the spiritual discipline of petitionary prayer.

> ▸ St Ambrose considered sin as a wound and Communion as the medicine to heal that wound.

> ▸ Prayer is our impotence depending upon his omnipotence.

- Prayer is not about feeling good, but about being transformed by the renewal of our minds.
- Too often we pray for a change in our circumstances when what is needed is a change in our character.
- *When I pray coincidences happen, and when I don't, they don't.*
**William Temple**

## () **Closing prayer**

*Father,*
We thank you for being with us this evening.
We thank you for the bread and wine, which speak so powerfully to us of the Lord Jesus.
Thank you that through them you have poured your grace into our lives.
Thank you for your provision in our daily lives, that we want for no good thing.
We want to pray for our brothers and sisters who are struggling in difficult circumstances.
We pray that you will:

> provide food for those who are hungry,
> companionship for the lonely,
> comfort for those who grieve,
> healing for those who are sick,
> and guidance and direction for those who are lost.

We ask for all these things in the precious name of Jesus.
*Amen*

### Exodus 16:1-8, 13-18

*The whole Israelite community set out from Elim and came to the desert of Sin, which is between Elim and Sinai, on the fifteenth day of the second month after they had come out of Egypt.*

*In the desert the whole community grumbled against Moses and Aaron.*

*The Israelites said to them: 'If only we had died by the Lord's hand in Egypt! There we sat round pots of meat and ate all the food we wanted, but you have brought us out into this desert to starve this entire assembly to death.'*

*Then the Lord said to Moses: 'I will rain down bread from heaven for you. The people are to go out each day and gather enough for that day. In this way I will test them and see whether they will follow my instructions. On the sixth day they are to prepare what they bring in, and that is to be twice as much as they gather on the other days.'*

*So Moses and Aaron said to all the Israelites: 'In the evening you will know that it was the Lord who brought you out of Egypt, and in the morning you will see the glory of the Lord, because he has heard your grumbling against him. Who are we, that you should grumble against us?'*

*Moses also said: 'You will know that it was the Lord when he gives you meat to eat in the evening and all the bread you want in the morning, because he has heard your grumbling against him. Who are we? You are not grumbling against us, but against the Lord.'*

*That evening quail came and covered the camp, and in the morning there was a layer of dew around the camp.*

*When the dew was gone, thin flakes like frost on the ground appeared on the desert floor.*

*When the Israelites saw it, they said to each other: 'What is it?' for they did not know what it was.*

*Moses said to them: 'It is the bread the Lord has given you to eat. This is what the Lord has commanded. Each one is to gather as much as he needs. Take an omer for each person you have in your tent.'*

*The Israelites did as they were told; some gathered much, some little. And when they measured it by the omer, he who gathered much did not have too much, and he who gathered little did not have too little.*

*Each one gathered as much as he needed.*

**Forgiveness in action**

▸ In 1987 the IRA exploded a massive car bomb in Enniskillen. One of those killed was the young daughter of Gordon Wilson, a committed Christian. Shortly after her death he said: 'I miss my daughter and we shall miss her, but I bear no ill will, I bear no grudge.'

▸ In August 1993 Amy Biehl, a young American student undertaking charity work, was killed in a political riot in the township of Guguletu on the outskirts of Cape Town. Four young men were found guilty of her murder and were sentenced to 18 years in prison. As a result of Desmond Tutu's wonderful experiment – the Truth and Reconciliation Commission – the young men were granted amnesty. Two of them now work for the Amy Biehl Foundation, established by her parents in memory of their daughter. Amy's mother says: 'Amy lives on in these two.'

▸ In January 2003 policeman Steven Oake was stabbed to death while detaining a suspect in Manchester. His family were shattered by his death, none more so than his parents. His father Robin, a retired police officer and committed Christian, spoke shortly after his death, saying: 'I am praying hard for the fellow who stabbed Steve. I am trying hard to forgive him as I am sure Steve would . . . I don't want any recriminations against him at all.'

**Personal notes relating to session four** | **Key Bible verses**

# Forgive us our debts

*Forgive us our debts, as we also have forgiven our debtors.*
**Matthew 6:12**

 ## Aims

At the end of this session people should:

> ▸ have shared their thoughts about the newspaper article
> ▸ actively participated in a discussion
> ▸ have a deeper understanding of the parable of the two debtors and/or Paul's relationship with the Corinthians

 ## Background notes

### Section A

Jesus uses the Greek word *opheilema*, which means debt. This is based upon the Aramaic word *hoba*, which expresses the Hebrew concept of sin as a debt to God. The sense is that we have obligations to God and if we fail in those obligations we are in debt to him. Jesus is teaching us to keep short accounts with God.

In Luke's version of the prayer he uses the Greek word *harmartia*, which is translated as sin with the thought of missing the mark.

This petition is not advocating a *quid pro quo*, whereby our forgiveness by God is somehow dependent upon our ability and willingness to forgive others. Rather, it is a prayer that from God's forgiveness of us will flow our forgiveness to others. Our experience of God's forgiveness leads naturally to the development of a forgiving spirit in us. Neither should we wait until we feel forgiveness. If we feel anger or resentment then we must bring these things to God as part of our prayer. Prayer has its own internal logic and God will deal with our feelings as part of the reciprocal nature of prayer. Forgiveness is a package deal.

Wrongs, real or imagined, can lock us into a prison of resentment, bitterness, or just a general malaise of feeling hard done by. Failure to forgive one another is not just a matter of failing to live up to some grandiose exhortation, but is a fundamental flaw in the human condition, a denial of our basic humanity.

Here the Lord's Prayer binds two aspects of prayer together:

> ▸ A petition: 'Forgive us . . .'

> ▸ An action to complement the petition: 'As we forgive . . .'

Our praying and our behaving are here locked indissolubly together. Such a linking challenges us to constantly explore the relationship between our asking and our acting. And yet we are not talking about some *quid pro quo* arrangement whereby our forgiveness is quantitively determined by the level of our forgiveness of others. The lesson is more fundamental and nuanced than such a superficial equation. Our forgiveness of others flows naturally from our experiences of being forgiven. Our experience of God determines the way we behave, our 'works' are a natural expression of our 'faith'. Our living relationship with God impacts upon every aspect of our lives.

How do you handle a developing sense of dislike or resentment against somebody, or even just a creeping sense of indifference? It is not just a matter of feeling. It can be desperately difficult, if not close to impossible, to change your feelings by willing to do so. The simplest solution is to pray for the person who is the object of our indifference, dislike or resentment. Through prayer God in his grace acts on our lives and we learn to love one another. This love is not sloppy sentimentality but rather a respect, a mutual regard, and a genuine desire for the welfare of the other person. When we take this prayer seriously it becomes an integral part of our lifestyle, determining the quality of our relationships and liberating us from bondage to negative attitudes and simmering resentment. It is not an optional bolt-on element to our lives, but the very heartbeat of our being, what one writer calls an amnesty of the heart.

This is the only petition that Jesus goes on to comment upon, see Matthew 6:14-15.

One of the best commentaries on this petition is the parable of the unforgiving servant (Matthew 18:23-35) and Jesus' response to Peter's query in Matthew 18:22.

Some people – as they grow older – experience a deepening sense of failure, inadequacy, and a feeling that they represent nothing more than plain, spiritual mediocrity. This is an example of how easy it is for sin to dominate our lives, or how easy it is to suddenly be overwhelmed by some sudden sin. Our awareness of the need for forgiveness should grow daily as we become more sensitive to how far short of God's high calling we fall, and a growing sense of our need for forgiveness should lead to a growing willingness and commitment on our part to forgive others.

## Section B
Paul and the Corinthians.
These notes are provided to support Activity 6.

### Corinth
▸ Crossroads of travel and commerce
▸ Destroyed in 146 BC but re-established by Julius Caesar as a Roman colony in 44 BC
▸ Provincial capital of Achaia
▸ Residence of the proconsul – Acts 18:12; 2 Corinthians 1:1
▸ Home to the Isthmian Games, second only in importance to the Olympic Games
▸ Biggest city Paul had yet visited
▸ Cosmopolitan population not unlike a modern inner city
▸ Towering over the city was the Acrocorinth, a hill nearly 2000 feet high with a temple to Aphrodite on the top. More than 1000 priestesses who were also ritual prostitutes
▸ Adjacent to two very busy seaports

> A large temple to Apollo and Corinth became a centre for homosexuality
> Renowned for its immorality – one of the Greek words for 'to commit fornication' was *korinthiazomai*
> Numerous banqueting halls attached to temples have been found in Corinth
> A plethora of cults claiming miracles, healings, ecstatic prophecies, interpreting of prophecies, and visions
> Paul came to Corinth with 'much fear and trembling'!

Are these facts about Corinth reflected at all in Paul's letters to the church?

### Paul and the Church in Corinth

> Founded by Paul during his second missionary journey – Acts 18:1-17. Paul stayed for about 18 months. He worked as a leather worker, making tents to pay his way, a fact that would not have endeared him to the more elitist amongst the Corinthians
> Had a shared ministry with Priscilla and Aquilla
> Gallio proconsul *c.* AD 51-53
> Paul then moved on to Ephesus where he stayed for about three years.

While in Ephesus Paul writes to the Corinthians about sexual immorality. We no longer have this letter but it is referred to in 1 Corinthians 5:9-10, and some scholars believe that 2 Corinthians 6:14-7:1 is part of that letter. The church in Corinth then write to Paul with a series of questions about a variety of issues, and Paul also receives oral reports of divisions in the church.

Paul responds by writing 1 Corinthians and addressing a range of issues including:

> Divisions
> Their rather blasé attitude to sexual matters
> Internal disputes

▸ A refusal to consider the needs of 'weaker brethren'

▸ Spiritual gifts

Paul then makes an unscheduled visit to Corinth from Ephesus (AD 54)

The visit does not go well. He is publicly insulted and his authority challenged.

The Church fails to back him in this confrontation and the situation is made worse by visiting preachers, who also challenge his authority.

Paul leaves in great disappointment.


In AD 55 Paul sends a letter of severe rebuke via Titus. Some scholars believe 2 Corinthians, chapters 10-13 is this letter.

Titus returns with good news. They have responded to the rebuke, although some still criticise Paul for apparently being fickle, and Jewish Christian preachers are still trying to take advantage of the immature Corinthians and seeking to undermine Paul's authority and threatening to lead the Church astray.

Nevertheless, Paul is encouraged, sends 2 Corinthians, chapters 1-9 as a letter of reconciliation but with echoes of the problems still detectable in his writing.

Many of Paul's problems with the Corinthians stemmed from the fact that even though Corinth as a whole, and therefore probably the Church, had a real mix of people from different socio-economic backgrounds, there was a strong core of powerful and wealthy people. Social climbing was an art form in Corinth and some of these social climbers were influential church members. By contrast, Paul insisted on paying his way by working with his hands making leather tents.

Well-to-do and aristocratic Romans had a low impression of common artisans and would have been upset and alienated by Paul deliberately identifying himself as one of the workers. They expected Paul to cut an impressive figure – eloquent, sophisticated, smart, and status-conscious. Instead they got Paul, the humble servant to whom public speaking did not come naturally, and who was probably pretty unprepossessing in appearance.

The challenge for Paul was to forge a strong moral and theological identity for the Church in Corinth, while generating a sense of belonging and commitment on the part of a really mixed group of people.

Summary of Paul's correspondence with the Corinthians:

- ▸ Letter 1:    Concerning sexual immorality.
                 Possibly 2 Corinthians 6:14-7:1
- ▸ Letter 2:    1 Corinthians
- ▸ Letter 3:    Strong letter of rebuke.
                 Possibly 2 Corinthians 10-13
- ▸ Letter 4.    Letter of reconciliation. 2 Corinthians 1-9

 ## Resources

- ▸ Paper, pens/pencils
- ▸ Flipchart and pens
- ▸ Filing cards to write on
- ▸ Waste paper bin
- ▸ Bibles

 ## Activities

1   Each person shares what phrase/sentence they underlined in the newspaper article and say something about it. Just two minutes each. Room here for moving into a discussion on how we would react, etc.

2   How hard is it to forgive? What are the barriers to forgiving? Why do we hold on to grudges, resentments?

3   Is our forgiveness dependent upon our forgiving? If we are not in a right relationship with other people (horizontal relationships), how does that affect our relationship with God (vertical relationship)?

4   The parable of the two debtors, Matthew 18:23-35. Read the story together. Agree an appropriate headline to sum up the

main part of the story. Underneath the headline, record the four or five key points which help us understand the parable. List the other pieces of key information which round out our understanding and appreciation of what Jesus is teaching.

5   A time of prayer, during which you give people the opportunity to write on a card some issue, feeling or experience which is holding them back in their walk with God. Invite them to write it out, reflect or pray silently about it, and then tear it up and put it in the bin (which you have thoughtfully provided!).

6   Case study. Paul and the Corinthians. This session is designed to increase knowledge and understanding of the Bible and to move from a part of the session with a significant emotional element into a different atmosphere. Attached you will find outline notes to be presented crisply and clearly, outlining Paul's relationship with the Corinthians emphasising how badly they treated him. Then together read 2 Corinthians 2:1-10. Summarise Paul's attitude to those who had given him such a hard time.

## Points to ponder

▸ *Put away from you all bitterness and wrath and anger and wrangling and slander, together with all malice, and be kind to one another, tender-hearted, forgiving one another, as God in Christ has forgiven you.* **Ephesians 4:31-32**

▸ Ravensbruck was a Nazi concentration camp specifically for women and children. Here, women and children were routinely abused, tortured, murdered, and ill-treated. More than 90,000 perished in the camp. When liberated, a prayer was found written on a scrap of paper near the body of a dead child.

*O Lord*
Remember not only the men and women of goodwill,
but also those of illwill.
But do not only remember the suffering they have
inflicted on us,
remember the fruits we bought, thanks to this suffering.
Our comradeship, our loyalty, our humility,
the courage, the generosity,
the greatness of heart which has grown out of all this,
and when they come to judgement
let all the fruits that we have borne be their forgiveness.
*Amen*

▸ The love we bear to others is the mark of authenticity of our faith.

▸ To fail to forgive is to create a prison for ourselves, to inflict a mortal wound upon our lives. Only in forgiveness is there freedom, healing and wholeness.

▸ *Therefore, my beloved brethren, be steadfast, immovable, and always abounding in the work of the Lord, knowing that in the Lord your labour is not in vain.* **1 Corinthians 15:58**

▸ *I have been driven many times to my knees by the overwhelming conviction that I had nowhere else to go. My own wisdom, and that of all about me, seemed insufficient for the day.* **Abraham Lincoln**

▸ If there are things in our life we feel we cannot pray about, then we should seriously consider whether they ought to be in our lives at all.

## () Closing prayer

*Lord, make me an instrument of your peace.*
*Where there is hatred, let me sow love;*
*where there is injury, pardon;*
*where there is doubt, faith;*
*where there is despair, hope;*
*where there is darkness, light;*
*and where there is sadness, joy.*

*O Divine Master, grant that I may not so much seek*
*to be consoled as to console,*
*to be understood as to understand*
*to be loved as to love.*
*For it is in giving that we receive,*
*it is in pardoning that we are pardoned,*
*and it is in dying that we are born to eternal life.*
**St Francis of Assisi**

| Personal notes relating to session five | Key Bible verses |
| --- | --- |
| | |

# And lead us not into temptation

*And lead us not into temptation, but deliver us from the evil one.*
**Matthew 6:13**

## Aims

At the end of this session people should:

▸ Understand what the Bible says about going through trying times
▸ Be better equipped to cope with such times
▸ Share with and support one another
▸ Have a deeper understanding of the experience of Job and/or the story of David and Bathsheba

## Background notes

Part of the problem with this petition is the thought that God leads us into temptation. Canadian scholar Dr Donald A. Carson sees this petition as a litotes. That is a figure of speech which 'expresses something by negating the contrary'. He quotes as an example Jesus' words, 'All that the Father gives to me, and whoever comes to me I will never drive away.' In other words if you come to Jesus he will bend over backwards to keep you. So Carson reads this petition as a litotes and suggests we read it as 'Lead us not into temptation, but away from it, into righteousness, into situations where, far from being tempted, we will be protected.'

Others see it as a prayer for God not to lead us into times and/or circumstances of testing, recognising that they are nevertheless a part of life, an integral part of the human condition. The Greek word *peirasmos* can be translated as 'temptation' or 'testing' dependent upon the context. Thus it becomes a prayer not to be tested beyond our endurance. Testing is part of the normal Christian experience, but we pray here that we will not be taken beyond our capacity to cope with it, in other words to be delivered from evil (or the evil one, as the Greek can also be translated).

The final clause makes it clear that it is Satan who tests/tempts us. The classic example is where God allows Job to be tested in order to strengthen Job's faith and to provide a wonderful witness to God's power and graciousness. Yet the book as a whole does more than view suffering merely as an instrument of discipline. It asserts that there is an underlying mystery to the suffering of the innocent, a mystery which is not solvable by human rationality.

Nevertheless it is clear from scripture that suffering, testing and temptation have the potential to be strongly educative. They have a purpose, to produce in us endurance which builds our character as Christian people. One of the biblical metaphors for this is that of refining:

'In this you rejoice, even if now for a little while you have had to suffer various trials, so that the genuineness of your faith – being more precious than gold that, though perishable is tested by fire – may be found to result in praise and glory and honour when Jesus Christ is revealed.' 1 Peter 1:6-7

The experience of the Christian is very real in terms of feeling stronger, closer to God, and more able to be a disciple if and when temptation is successfully resisted or testing endured positively and prayerfully. It is a natural part of our Christian life requiring a determined act of willpower, but so is the reality of God's grace.

Paul really appreciated the temptations facing the Corinthian Christians: immorality, pride, divisiveness, spiritual superiority and error; but he tells them that God will not test them to destruction. He always provides sufficient strength to be victorious. 1 Corinthians 10:13 is a verse worth learning off by heart: 'No testing has overtaken you that is not common to everyone. God is faithful, and he will not let you be tested beyond your strength, but with the testing he will also provide the way out so that you may be able to endure it.'

And because Paul recognised that successful resistance leads to growth in Christian character and maturity he could talk about rejoicing in testing:

'. . . we also boast in our sufferings, knowing that suffering produces endurance, and endurance produces character, and character produces hope, and hope does not disappoint us, because God's love has been poured into our heart through the Holy Spirit that has been given unto us.' Romans 5:3-5

Some years ago my younger brother suddenly died. He was young, successful, had a young family, and until then had been literally full of life. Christian friends wrote to me a letter full of traditional evangelical platitudes which were of no comfort at all. Theology is small comfort in times of intense grief. Another friend simply sent me a copy of the quote from Mother Julian (see page 76). It made all the difference. The hurt, pain, anger and frustration were all still there, but God had said: 'Thou shalt not be overcome!'

## Job

These notes are provided in support of Activity 2.

What would Job have made of the quote on page 71? Job was a man renowned for his righteousness. In chapter one of his book he is described as blameless and upright, fearing God and shunning evil.

Certainly, Job's early life would have given credence to the notion that righteousness produces wealth and prosperity. Job was a wealthy man with an enviable lifestyle. And yet early in the story the scene shifts to heaven, where Satan confronts God and challenges God's confidence in Job's altruistic goodness. Satan suggests that the only reason Job is godly, is because he is so well looked after. He can afford to be godly because life is so good for him. But remove Job's wealth and things will be very different – according to Satan.

'Does Job fear God for nothing? Have you not put a fence around him and his house and all that he has, on every side? You have blessed the work of his hands, and his possessions have increased in the land. But stretch out your hand now, and touch all that he has, and he will curse you to your face.' Job 1:9-11

In response to Satan's challenge God allows Satan to test Job's commitment. Job loses his wealth and his family, all the things he held most dear, and yet he sustains his righteousness. Nevertheless, Job recognises that all he has, God has given, and God has the right to take it away. Job is not going to renege on his commitment to the Lord in the face of such testing.

Satan decides to up the ante. Job has lost his family and his possessions, but he still has his health. Touch Job in person and things will surely be different. It will be impossible for Job to sustain his integrity.

Job now enters the next stage of his 'testing' in which he loses both his health and the support of his wife, and yet he stands firm:

'In all this Job did not sin with his lips.' Job 2:10

To all intents and purposes it is clear that Job's piety is not dependent upon his prosperity. Job quietly acquiesces to the will of God and to all intents and purposes the story appears to be over. Job accepts the will of God for his life and in so doing becomes a model for all who suffer.

Nevertheless we soon learn that Job feels a great deal more than he is saying, and we move into the second part of the book, in which Job moves from apparently serene acceptance of his condition to one of assertive questioning. Here we encounter a turbulent Job whose mind is in turmoil, deep in a sense of alienation and with a strong sense of having been unfairly treated.

In this second section of the book Job's three friends seek to make sense of Job's suffering in the light of their fundamental belief that such suffering is a sign of God's displeasure. God is punishing sin, or at the very least providing a strong warning against sin! In their different ways the 'friends' seek to give a different nuance to the theory of divine retribution:

Eliphaz maintains that the suffering may well not be permanent. Bildad maintains that Job must have sinned but it isn't so bad as he is still alive!

Zophar maintains that Job must have been a secret sinner of some significance to be punished so severely, but there is an element of mercy in God as Job still lives!

To Job the theological speculations of his friends appear spurious. Throughout their speeches Job maintains his innocence, not in an egotistical self-pitying fashion, but resolutely challenging God to justify his treatment of his servant.

Elihu appears on the scene and provides another perspective – that suffering is the vehicle of God's revelation. By this time Job is silent. Although Elihu speaks four times, Job does not respond. It is as if he has made his case and he is now waiting to hear from God. And in chapter 38 God responds, not by providing a logical and sequential explanation as to why the innocent suffer, but by asking Job a series of fundamental questions. These questions have the effect of reminding Job that he is a mere man, whereas God is the Creator and Sustainer of the Universe.

The questions roll out of heaven like some divine, cosmic CV and they go on and on – all reminding Job of who God is. Here is an echo of Jeremiah's picture of God as the potter and the human being a mere lump of clay. Locked into all these questions is a subtle and sophisticated comparison of the natural order with the moral order. Just as Job does not understand the ways of Behemoth and Leviathan, hippopotamus and crocodile, so too Job does not understand the workings of the moral order. Just as there is much that is incomprehensible in the world of nature, so it is with the moral order. Just as you cannot understand the hippopotamus, so you cannot understand innocent suffering. The only sense it makes, it makes to God. Such things are not amenable to human rationality.

God knows what he is doing and is under no obligation to explain himself to man.

Job's response? He is satisfied.

'I know that you can do all things, and that no purpose of yours can be thwarted . . . I had heard of you by the hearing of the ear, but now my eye sees you; therefore I despise myself, and repent in dust and ashes.' Job 42:2, 5-6

Job's experience of God now becomes his theology. I thought I knew you, but really I only understood less than half. What I did know was real, but it was nowhere near enough, it was nowhere near the whole truth. The whole truth is that ultimately you are unknowable, your ways are past understanding, you are beyond mere intellectual analysis, it is enough to know that you are.

The problem of innocent suffering retains a strong element of mystery. Ultimately the problem of pain is not totally reducible to rational explanation. A significant slice of mystery remains. This element does not mean a stoic resignation but an embracing of the experience for it is here we will find God.

## David and Bathsheba

These notes are provided in support of Activity 6.

If somebody said to me: 'Which Old Testament character would you like to be?' I would be tempted to say: 'David!' He had everything going for him. He was:

> Tall, dark, and handsome;
>
> A fearless warrior;
>
> A devoted friend with strong interpersonal skills;
>
> An outstanding intellect;
>
> A poet of extraordinary skill and sensitivity;
>
> Able to play musical instruments;
>
> A powerful, prestigious, and popular leader . . .
>
> And he could probably play football!

Above all, he was a deeply spiritual man, one of God's chosen men, a veritable pillar of the church. And yet in a moment of strong temptation he failed (2 Samuel 11:1-27).

David would have had a good view of his city from the roof of his palace. Yet should he not have been away with the army leading them in the campaign against the Amalekites? The Amalekites had been a persistent thorn in Israel's side. Time and again they had attacked Israel. Surely such a well-established and persistent enemy required David's full attention? Was this a case of the devil finding work for idle hands? How much more vulnerable are we when tired, idle, or just plain fed up?

Was Bathsheba a willing accomplice or a victim? Did she know David was looking? Did she deliberately go out of her way to be seen? What should David have done the moment he saw her?

How does Uriah's behaviour contrast with that of David? Interestingly, it is emphasised that Uriah was a Hittite, not a native Israelite, and yet his name means 'Yahweh is my light'.

Why was David so intent on getting Uriah home to sleep with his wife? Why did Uriah obstinately resist? What does this tell us of his character? One writer comments: 'Uriah drunk is more pious than David sober.' Why was David so intent on having Uriah killed?

David seems more intent on preserving his own reputation than with his failure to uphold God's standards of conduct and behaviour.

Think about the repercussions of David's failure to deal with temptation.

 ## Resources

> ▸ Photocopies of the quote on page 71.
> ▸ Flipchart and pens.
> ▸ Photocopy Bible references on pages 72-75, mount on card and circulate to members of the group.

 ## Activities

1   Ask each member of the group to say which Old Testament character they would like to be and to say why.

2   Perhaps not many would wish to be Job. Talk through the story of Job with discussion of the questions at various points. In what way was Job tested and how did he do in the test?

3   Provide everybody with a copy of the quote on page 71. What do we think of this quotation? Get people to discuss in pairs for about five minutes, and then group pairs into fours to compare views, and then bring everybody together for a summing up.

4   Split into small groups to discuss personal experience of testing. How did people cope? What was most difficult?

What helped? What was learned? How did people change? What would they do differently next time? Provide each group with the Bible quotations on card. What are the key learning points from these verses?

5   Regroup to share views.

6   As a group share what people know about the story of David and Bathsheba. Build the story up using a large flipchart sheet, and then either as a whole group or in small groups discuss the key questions. Contrast David's failure to cope with temptation, with Job's response to severe testing in his life.

7   Conclude with a time of prayer and ministry, seeking God's help to overcome temptation and to stand firm in the face of difficult circumstances.

## Oh really . . . ?

God has a brilliant plan for each of our lives. This plan includes a well-paid job, a nice home, and a trouble-free family life.

If our lives are troubled, dull and unsuccessful it is because we have not been what God wants us to be. If we have a sense of failure, of personal pointlessness, and our hearts feel hard and cold, it is not God's fault. Personal prosperity is dependent upon our faithfulness.

If we are faithful, all doors will open to us, all obstacles will disappear, and we will have plenty of money, and be ecstatically happy. The Bible promises personal prosperity for the faithful Christian.

### Colossians 1:9-14

Paul, right at the beginning of this letter to the church in Colossae, says much about his praying for them, and what he expects his prayers to achieve in their lives:

Ceaseless prayer that they might be:
1. Filled with:
> ‣ knowledge
>
> ‣ wisdom
>
> ‣ spiritual understanding
>> (*in order to live lives worthy of the Lord*)

2. Strong and patient:
> ‣ to endure hardship
>> (*which produces character*)

. . . And all this to be characterised by thankfulness because:
> ‣ God has rescued them from darkness
>
> ‣ They now have an inheritance
>
> ‣ They are part of Christ's kingdom
>> (*these are objective realities, giving*
>> *Christians a different perspective*)

### James 1:2-3

In this passage James emphasises the importance of prayer as our lifeline to God when the going gets tough. He goes on to remind his readers of God's generosity – reminding us that God gives ungrudgingly in response to our asking. James uses a number of interesting words:

*Peirasmos:* testing, a trial or temptation specifically with the purpose of producing a stronger, purer person. A young child learning to walk, tests his legs. In the Old Testament the queen of Sheba came to Solomon to test his wisdom.

*Dokimion:* this is the process of testing, and is the word for genuine coins that are unadulterated by impurities. The impure substances have been burnt out.

*Hupomone:* patient endurance, not in a passive grudging mode, but embracing the trial in order to get something out of it.

*Teleios:* mature, fit for the purposes God has called us to.

*Holokleros:* complete, perfect in every part, without imperfection.

*Leipesthai:* deficient in nothing, victorious.

## 2 Corinthians 1:3-4

Paul is glad to have experienced the strength given by God through innumerable trials and tribulations. As a result of his experiences he is able to empathise with the difficulties faced by the churches he founded. His experience of consolation, comfort and encouragement is now something he shares with others. Genuine sympathy can only stem from experience, it cannot be generated with our minds but will stem from our hearts. Paul is not an aloof intellectual writing an abstract theological treatise but a man who shares deeply in the experiences of the people for whom he has pastoral responsibility. He is well versed in the 'school of hard knocks'; it does not make him bitter or resentful but brings out genuine care and compassion for others.

## Hebrews 12:5-7

The writer to the Hebrews brings fresh perceptions to the problem of suffering. Difficult times can shake our faith, produce uncertainty, plunge us into despair, or make us angry and resentful. But for the Christian they can be a sign of our filial relationship with the Father. They are a proof of our sonship, or daughtership. Properly understood we see them as times of training when God is taking us on into a deeper appreciation of our faith and as such should stimulate our confidence and provide us with a sense of dignity as children of God. When facing hardship there is a natural tendency to look inwards and to feel sorry for ourselves. We need to remind ourselves that such times do stem from the love and grace of God and are a token of our sonship/daughtership.

**Deuteronomy 8:2**

God tested and trained the children of Israel in the wilderness. Having left Egypt under the leadership of Moses it was not until a generation later that they began to move into the Promised Land under the leadership of Joshua. During that time in the desert their relationship with God was something of a rollercoaster, times of disobedience and defiance interspersed with God's miraculous intervention in the life of the people. Yet throughout this period there is a strong sense of purpose in God's dealings with the Israelites.

What sort of times and/or experiences could be described as a 'wilderness' for us?

What circumstances could be described as putting us to the test?

What lessons can we learn from such times?

**Points to ponder**

> *Bend us, O Lord,*
> *where we are hard and cold,*
> *in your refiner's fire:*
> *come purify the gold.*
> **Graham Kendrick and Chris Rolinson**

> The goal of the Christian life is not enlightenment but wholeness.

> *Pray to God in the storm but keep on rowing.* **Danish proverb**

> *Prayer is a shield to the soul, a sacrifice to God, and a scourge to Satan.* **John Bunyan**

> *God promises a safe landing but not a calm passage.* **Bulgarian proverb**

> *He said not: 'Thou shall not be tempested, thou shall not be travailed, thou shall not be dis-eased'; but he said: 'Thou shall not be overcome.'* **Mother Julian**

> *Before I was humbled I went astray, but now I keep your word.* **Psalm 119:67**

> *Kneel before you leap.* **George H. Allen**

> *It is quite useless knocking at the door of heaven for earthly comfort; it's not the sort of comfort they supply there.* **C. S. Lewis**

> When we pray we enter a world in which God and evil battle for supremacy in our lives.

## ( ) Closing prayer

*Heavenly Father,*

Be my light:
  guide me when lost
  clarify my confusions
  enlighten me when I do not understand
  and lead me in your everlasting ways.

Be my shield:
  protect me from evil
  guard my heart from deception
  let me not be overwhelmed by my frailties.

Be my hope:
  encourage me when life just seems too
   much
  lift me up when I feel low
  enrich me when I feel spiritually and
   mentally impoverished.

Be my purpose:
  bring a sense of meaning and direction to
   my life
  each day may I be aware of your guiding
   and leading in every aspect of my life.

Father, break through all the walls I have erected
and reign supreme in every aspect of my being.

Through Jesus Christ, your Son our Saviour.
*Amen*

| Personal notes relating to session six | Key Bible verses |
| --- | --- |
| | |

# Questionnaire I

## Leader's self-assessment and feedback
## (can also be used for group member feedback)

Circle the number which best represents your view of how effective you are (or your leader is, if you are a group member providing feedback) in each item, e.g. I indicates that you acknowledge you (or your leader) need(s) to work at something, while 5 indicates that you think you are good at it (or your leader is good at it).

| | | | | | |
|---|---|---|---|---|---|
| Relating to people | I | 2 | 3 | 4 | 5 |
| Creating a warm, friendly atmosphere | I | 2 | 3 | 4 | 5 |
| Prayer | I | 2 | 3 | 4 | 5 |
| Asking questions | I | 2 | 3 | 4 | 5 |
| Studying the passage/materials | I | 2 | 3 | 4 | 5 |
| Encouraging people | I | 2 | 3 | 4 | 5 |
| Facilitating rather than dominating | I | 2 | 3 | 4 | 5 |
| Comfortable with silence | I | 2 | 3 | 4 | 5 |
| Handling disagreements | I | 2 | 3 | 4 | 5 |
| Including everybody | I | 2 | 3 | 4 | 5 |
| Keeping in contact | I | 2 | 3 | 4 | 5 |
| Handling difficult situations | I | 2 | 3 | 4 | 5 |
| Motivating people to take part | I | 2 | 3 | 4 | 5 |
| Listening | I | 2 | 3 | 4 | 5 |

*Areas I need to pray about:*

*Actions I can take:*

*Things to work on:*

*My experience of the home group:*

# Questionnaire 2

## Group member feedback

Your group leader would like to know your views on this study series. Circle the number which best represents your views, e.g. 1 indicates that you disagree strongly, while 5 indicates that you agree strongly.

| | | | | | |
|---|---|---|---|---|---|
| Our group has a warm, relaxed, friendly feel to it | 1 | 2 | 3 | 4 | 5 |
| Everybody is encouraged to take part | 1 | 2 | 3 | 4 | 5 |
| The group has helped me grow as a Christian | 1 | 2 | 3 | 4 | 5 |
| I enjoy the Bible study sessions in my group | 1 | 2 | 3 | 4 | 5 |
| The leader of my group is a good listener | 1 | 2 | 3 | 4 | 5 |
| I look forward to going to the group | 1 | 2 | 3 | 4 | 5 |
| I feel encouraged by my group | 1 | 2 | 3 | 4 | 5 |
| No one person dominates the group | 1 | 2 | 3 | 4 | 5 |
| Social activities are an important part of the group | 1 | 2 | 3 | 4 | 5 |
| Inputs are stimulating and interesting | 1 | 2 | 3 | 4 | 5 |

*Comments:*